A CALLING OUT TO NUBIA

poetry for the young and old.

A

CALLING OUT TO

NUBIA

poetry for the young and old.

Indigo K. Bethea

ISBN: 0-75960-133-X

This book is printed on acid free paper.

1stBooks - rev. 2/14/01

This book of words is dedicated to my mother Joanne Bethea, my great-grandmother Dora Staley, my aunts, uncles, cousins, friends, and neighbors, for their contributions to my education, knowledge of my Creator, and knowledge of self.

I would like to thank the following people: Dr. Susan Gotsch, Mrs. Nejla Camponeschi, Dr. Connie Anderson, Dr. Michael Woost, and Dr. Adrian McFarlane. These people were crucial to my development as an undergraduate. In their own ways, they each challenged me to rise to the occasion--and showed me how.

Foreword

A Calling Out to Nubia is a collection of poems which spans almost a decade of Ms. Bethea's development and socio-political consciousness. The reader will find in these poems a cornucopia of cultural pride [e.g. ***True Pride***], bold iconoclastic anti-Black stereotypes [section entitled ***Beauty***], uplifting celebrations of personhood [e.g. ***In the Shadow of a Slave***], community pride [e.g. ***Not a Ghetto…Home***], introspective journeys inside the [self]"hood", and an unapologetic affirmation of salutary images of the self [e.g. ***Dolly Dolly*** and ***Mirror, Mirror***]. It is important to note that Ms. Bethea probably had no conceptual tools to analyze the intuitions she had in her early teens when some of these poems were first written. However, it is reasonable to assert that her language skills, harmonized with her honest feelings about her observations and experiences, have succeeded in articulating a "world view", albeit culturally nuanced and attenuated, with pinpoint accuracy.

But why NUBIA? one might ask; why not Africana, Black people, Urban Youth or the Marginalized? Nubia means different things to different groups of diasporic Africans. An elderly Black civil rights "warrior" defines Nubia as "**N**egroes **U**nder **B**urden **I**n **A**merica". An economically successful critic of what she calls "the rhapsody of empty Black verbiage" defines it as "**N**ameless **U**rban **B**lacks **I**ll-begotten, **A**imless". But there is another group, represented by the indefatigable Ms. Bethea, inter alios, who has chosen to see beyond Black nihilism without sentimentalizing its harsh reality. These persons define Nubia as: **N**ational **U**rgency [for] **B**old **I**nnovative **A**ction in order to **N**urture **U**nity **B**eyond **I**solating **A**ctivities.

Their goal, it seems, is to arrive at a state of affairs which is **N**atural, **U**nique, **B**old, **I**ntelligent and **A**mbitious. If the others are as talented, disciplined, resourceful, positively realistic and honest as Ms. Bethea, then the *Call to Nubia* may yield responses for transformation.

African peoples in the Americas and elsewhere have sought to find and make connections with Africa ever since the slave trade began. As centuries passed, the search for identity shifted from repatriation to reconnection. With the break-up of families, language and nationalities (called "tribes" by colonizers), the act of finding one's roots, Alex Haley notwithstanding, became more and more improbable. Additionally, acculturation has made the offsprings of diasporic Africans strangers to their "kin" in the vast continent of Africa. The next best thing is to find the best known elements of Africa, elevate them, and then try to integrate them into the matrix of our self-image. So while the Rastafari celebrate the regality and alleged divinity of the late Emperor Haile Selassie 1 of Ethiopia as a counterpoint to British denigration of African identity [see **Chanting Down Babylon,** McFarlane, et.al., Temple University Press, 1998]. Ms. Bethea and others have appropriated stories of the ancient kingdom of Nubia with its regality, beauty, community, resourcefulness and independence. What is noteworthy is that Nubia is a desert region in the Nile Valley of southern Egypt and northern Sudan. In spite of desert conditions and European-imposed lines of division, Nubians thrived with pride. That the economic conditions of the Nuba people are at Third World standards is of less importance than the connection with their past. In short, diasporic Africans are in search of a PAST which can sustain their PRESENT and both inspire and invigorate them to regain their FUTURE!

The use of Nubia in Ms. Bethea's fascinating collection of poems is a deliberate use of poetic licence; it is a coded expression of the creative imagination. It is self-regulated by a provocative metaphorical network whose function is understood by a cultural template of urban life. The extent to which the elasticity holds largely depends on the stretch of one's imagination--by the consciousness of those who are prepared to be stretched by the generation of opportunities rather than the stretch of "bad times". Furthermore, Nubia is used by Ms. Bethea on four levels: (1) as a place which physically represents desert conditions of isolation and desolation; (2) as a challenge for devising means of productivity; (3) as a people of legendary pride; and (4) as a diasporic corollary for self-reliance and the pursuit of excellence.

It is this fourth level which gives warrant to Ms. Bethea's use of the term Nubia; it symbolizes the exile, neglect and harsh realities of the Nubian desert. But the ***Call***--the expression of the word (*logos*)--is an invocation of the best in our creative imagination: It is a call for order out of disorder. For example, that parents and children *rarely listen* to each other is no secret. This results in succeeding generations becoming more and more distant, secretive and insensitive to the inner hurts and needs of each other. Every "Call" is a civil substitute for a *shout* but, more important, it is a plea for caring and nurturing listeners. It takes mutual care, a disciplined will, ingenuity and community to reclaim the desert of alienated selfhood, and compromised communities. Communities overcrowded with scarred psyches which have been the convenient landfills for psyche-social toxic waste are the norm, rather than the exception. **A Calling Out to Nubia** is a call to action, to selfhood, neighborhood and indeed, to Life!

I salute Ms. Bethea for exemplifying the responses of independence and creativity which her poetry so eloquently conveys—her poetry is original, and so is the accompanying artwork! In this text, the word and the image combine together to form a dynamic message worth emulating.

I highly recommend this collection to the young and old alike as a means to explore the pride of Nubia within and among themselves!

Adrian Anthony McFarlane
Professor of Philosophy
Hartwick College

Table Of Contents

Introduction
Whut It Is

          Well now chil'ren
listen up good
there's a whole lotta stories
               you's bout ta hear
                         cause i'm talkin bout thangs
like my beautiful hair.

          now ya see, as i was comin
up through school
i took ta writin poetry
and lawd, if a new world didn't open up to me!

as i moved into high school
     i became more aware
                         of the plight
                         of the struggle
                         of my peoples
everywhere.

whut it is, that is,
what this here book is,
is a collection of some of the thoughts/emotions
i managed to get down on paper.

whut i want all of yawl to get outta
     this book
is pride in who you are
     pride foe yo skin
     pride foe yo culture

pride foe yo race
and pride foe that nose sittin on yo face.

and when you close this here book,
i want you to have questions
and seek answers to why things are
the way they is

and **that's** whut it is!

Nubian Man

Young Man
Aug, 2000

A Man

What am I,
but a man?
True, I am not what you wanted
me to be,
But I am still a man.
It is clear to me
that my ways are different,
my walk seems queer,
cuts and bruises may appear,
my words might sound strange
But I am no more than I should be.
I am all that I could ever be,
I am a man.

Nubian Brother

Is it time Nubian Brother
to
    respect, love, nurture
            your Nubian Woman Mother Sister
                Women?
Is it time Nubian Brother
to
    love, educate, develop
            your Nubian Daughter Son Child
                Children?

Is it time my delightfully Black-skinned Brother
to
    become
            Father Husband Man
                Men?

When is it time, Nubian Brother...
to pay homage to our ancestors
to regain your honor
to bring pride to our name
            to our creed?

When is it time?

In The Shadow Of A Slave

C'mon Black Man
raise your head,
give respect to the voices
of the dead,
do you hear them calling from their graves?
Those are the voices of the slave.

BLACK IS BEAUTIFUL!
Be strong and brave,
I will not hang my head with the
agony of the slave.

From my soul were you produced
and from your hands will you birth
my fruit.
I will not eat
I will not drink
I will not sleep
in the shadow of a slave.
Fight the ways of an unjust world.
Little Brother,
do not hinder
do not fade
do not let yourself stand
in the repression of a slave.

Doors

Doors closing behind you
Doors closing in front of you
They done locked you out
or better yet, locked you in.

They know of your greatness
They fear your greatness
In fact they're trying to erase this.

Doors closing in front of you
...running the streets
are you sure that's what you
wanted to be?
Doors closing behind you
...locked down in a prison cell
where you expected yourself to be.

Gangsta Indigo I

Gotta be hip
Gotta be cool,
what happens when you wind up dead
fool?
Gotta be ruff. Gotta come strapped.
Brother don't you see
it's just a trap?
Look down yo noses,
makin like you all hard
and when the sh*t hits the fan
ya crying for God.

Steada trying to get a hold
on a real somethin
you walking round
frontin with nothin

Busy busin a cap in somebody's a** for respect
you need ta start busin that intellect.

Gangsta Indigo II

Chronic in hand
just like the white man planned
Head to the ground
fienin fo a pound

Livin the life of a wanna-be gangsta

Got that slide in the hip
cock in yo grip

yo man, when you gonna get tired a that sh*t?

Strength

Queen
Spring 97

Belief

I can move
mountains
Place waters
drink seas.
I can, because I say I can.
I can
defy the racism
become someone great
lift up others.
I can, because I say I can.
I can
love myself
love others
teach self-love.
I can, because I say I can
and I can make you believe that I can
do anything
see everything
be something
and don't you go runnin round sayin
"she can't"
I can because **I** say I can.

Save Your Sorrow For My Grave

Lord knows we all have
troubles..even me.
I've suffered through love
and the hardships of man.
But do not say "I feel
sorrow for you"
Don't give me your pity
during the times
I birth tears.
That is not the way in which you are to
see me.
Be in awe of my
strength,
my endurance
I don't need your sorrow,
Hold it for my funeral
Cause I'm very much alive
with no need to mourn.
Smile with me
laugh with me
Be Alive!!
Call me conceited,
but consider me brave.
So please,
save your weeping
save your sorrow
for when I'm dead
and in the grave.

Not A Ghetto..Home

On the news, I'm
seeing them tell the
story about life
in the ghetto.
I'm listening to the radio
and people justa singin
bout the ghetto.
And I realize,
this place,

this ain't no ghetto,
it's home.
When you say Ghetto,
I think of someplace
poor, desolate, without hope--something ugly!
I ain't livin in no ghetto.
I live in a place filled
with hope.
Bright eyes being born every minute.
And I see beauty all around me
angry beauty
hateful beauty
bitter beauty
weary beauty
hopeful beauty
beauty beauty
And I see barbecues,
children eatin ices
and runnin wild
Churchgoers..

I see life full, vibrant
Alive.
No, not a ghetto...
home.

True Pride

I look at myself in the mirror
and I realize..
There is a pride so strong in my legs
sometimes it's hard to walk!
There is a defiance in my shoulders and arms,
Hating every minute of being covered up.
There is a fire in my breast
soo strong
till it hurts me to breathe!
There is a haughtiness in my hair,
refusing to be tamed
SHOUTING to be seen.
There is conceit in this nose
passion in this mouth
and stubbornness in these eyes.
There is a dance in my hips,
just try and imitate it's song!
This body of mine,
so proud and beautiful,
till it hurts me to dress in the morning!

First Impressions

When I come stormin through
ya door,
Be won over by the fact that
I'm not tryin to win you over.
I don't give a d*mn
if you don't remember my name.
Whether your memories of me
are explicit or vague
doesn't phase me at all.
Just know
that I came
that I am
and will continue to be
angry and happy
bitter and sweet
mad as the devil and glad to see ya.

My mind is not concerned with your first impressions of me,
Cause I'm livin for God,
and dying for me.
So walk on with your little opinions and thoughts.

Uplifting Of A Nation

It is with hope and love
    that I look to you,
the beauty of your skin
the brilliance of your hue.

To all of my people,
    rise above and beyond your shackles.
As you move towards the steeple,
    grasp the moon,
intoxicate yourselves
    with the stars.
Be steadfast and strong,
    Mercy's goodness will help you along.

Believe in yourself
        conceive, achieve,
reprieve from all hostilities towards the next man.
Sit him down, shake his hand
show him the trueness of woman and man.

My Pretty Little Ring

I got myself a pretty little ring
from Africa.
Hand Made!
A pure reflection of me.

When other people look at my ring,
They just laugh and say 'What she want with that cheap ole ring?'

Let me tell yawl about my ring.
The body is made of copper
entwined within copper,
like the color of my skin after I've bathed in the sun.

Its crown with beads of red and green and white,
kissed by the seas,
emitting its radiance.

Each and every bead showing
its magical beauty
A perfect reflection of me.
That's
My pretty African ring,
Hand Made!

That Much Better

Try to close my eyes,
that much better
shall I see.

Try to burn my books,
that much more
shall I learn.

Try to poison my food,
that much healthier
shall I be.

Try to torture my sleep,
that much better
shall I dream.

Try to stop my growth,
that much taller
shall I grow.

Try to hold me back,
that much farther
shall I go.

Try to close my eyes,
as I watch you reap
what you sow.

From My Window

From my window
I watch the children frolic
in the snow.
Lining the sidewalks like soldiers;
snowballs their weaponry.
I feel the love of these children,
and remember my people.
Without food to eat
or water to drink;
On our faces,
that smile has never ceased,
and in times of war
has brought us peace.

Don't Give Up

In your time of need
    you stand alone.
A confused heart in a constant roam
    seems as though you walk alone...
But don't give up. Never, ever give up!
Stand tall. Be strong.
Your Creator, my Savior will help you along.

We live our lives in such a crazy way
    hoping to see tomorrow's today.
Life throws a faith shaking blow.
            so much pain, so much sorrow.
But don't feel cheated, slighted, misled
or defeated.
Don't sulk or be bitter, hear what I say?
        Cause God never promised you forever and a day.
Remember to laugh,
                    Remember to smile,
things won't seem so bad after while.
        Drink what's offered in life's cup
        and remember
NEVER GIVE UP!!!

My Hands

These hands sho nuff smooth
like a baby's backside.

These hands,
known to soothe tears
My hands
sho nuff strong.
Once they get their grip,
they never let go.

My hands
can do anything
comb a peasy head
braid Black hair,
Lawd I 'clare
These hands
grew mountains
planted seas
can slap a man to his knees
if he so much as disrespects me.
can clap my psalms
give music to a Christian song.

These hands nursed my chile
These hands
can create can cry
can love and will some day die,
can hate
So now,
look at my hands

with fate
written all in them
look at my hands
feel,
see it's magic
These hands right here,
that can make
the sea
soothe a tear
nurse a chile
These hands
These hands
Lawd Lawd
these hands!

Family

Family
Spring 97

I Can Appreciate..

What words can I give you?
They could never,
never
reciprocate your love.
What words could I offer you,
You, who have given me life?
So faithfully, you support my dreams
share my agonies..
having suffered them already.
How self-lessly
you give to me
how self-ishly
I receive.

If I could remove
the thorns of
sadness and bitterness
that gnaws at thy heart,

If I could show you
all the love
you truly deserve..
it wouldn't be enough.

So yes mother, I can appreciate
all the love
you give
self-lessly.

Smiles

Everybody in our family has different smiles. My mother's smile is lopsidedly beautiful with curiosity, strength and weakness, all thrown in.

My smile is kinda crazy, with a dimple on my left cheek, and two other dimples at the corners of my mouth, forming two acute angles to my chin, my smile fast becoming my mother's.

My grandmother's smile always reminds me of the deep South, my picking apples off the trees, playing with my dog named Blacky, feeding my two pigs, Henry and Sally, and looking at that pretty horse named Beauty.

A lopsided smile, a southern smile, and a pretty horse I never got to ride.

Singing You A Spirit

I am singing you a spirit
        to help you along the path of....death.
The song will have your eyes,
big and brown,
                free from your self-inflicted toxins.
The spirit will carry your laughter,
your glory,
                your sin.
I will miss you,
                my song.
I will miss you,
                my spirit.
Walk your path,
                so I can sing you a spirit.

In A Hospital Bed

There you are,
lying in a hospital bed
about to die..
Always knew it would happen.
If you weren't in jail
you were in the hospital
and if you weren't in the hospital,
you didn't know us.
Now look at the grief,
you're the cause of all this!

Why didn't you take
care of yourself?
Why didn't you believe
that you deserved better?
Why did you fail?
Now look at you,
in a hospital bed
about to die.
Your family might not
be able to bury
you.
Your sisters can't sleep,
trapped in a constant
toss and turn.

And I,
I sleep well.
It's just waking up that's
hard,

Cause I know
                    you're lying in a hospital bed
about to die
      and there's nothing
I can do.

In Your Eyes

I know it hurts, hurts so bad
                    to let go
to regain your self control.
I saw the tears burn out of your eyes,
the pain out of your heart.
          Through your eyes, I've seen the world.
Everyday, as pain glazed pain;
you struggled to raise your children.
          Now take a look at your children;
with uncertainty in their eyes.
Never knowing what you know
Never seeing what you see.
          How does the world look in your eyes, where brown
          meets the blues,
with thousands of shapes and hues
questioning,
seeking,
searching,
     yearning for your wisdom?

I hold so much respect for you Mothers and Fathers,
how strong you are in your will to survive!
How you can sacrifice for others with disregard for your own needs.
How those beautiful eyes shine,
when the world turns dangerous and hateful. How you managed to laugh, when you wanted to cry.
I feel the warmth radiating from your eyes, as you reminisce on yester-days and years.

Yes my Beautiful Mothers, My Beautiful Fathers;
I've seen the world through your eyes,
and it is quite an exquisite place!

Once Again

I wish we could all be together
once again
I wish time would slow it's pace
so that we could relive
    the days in which we cried
and laughed.
My God! How time has passed!
    I remember your smiling face,
as I helped you grow with grace.
I still see the pain in your heart,
as our lives were torn apart.
    I add this
to the days I've cried since.
        In my mind I review the
                events
that took us from one another.
And I cry to our Father, Who art
in Heaven;
Why curse us?
    It was you who nursed us!
I wish we could all be together...
    once again.

Youth

"Fear, Worry, Anger: The Three Emotions"
by I. K. B. Nov, 2000

You Wonder Why

In this world there is so much pain.
In this world, we struggle to be heard.
We have so many fears
so many worries.

And you wonder, how can there be so much hate?
And you wonder why we as a nation
act the way we do?
Well, I'll tell you why.
We feel so alone,

unheard
unseen
unthought of in this world.

We cry our pains,
our agonies..through crime
through drugs
even through violence
Because that is the only way we are heard....
There were many nights
when I cried,
How can we move forward
when so many try to hold us back?
You wanna know how to stop
the racism
the hatred
the anguish?
Listen to us. REALLY HEAR US.
Know that we are many

but our knowledge limited
our voices few.
Teach us.
Guide us.
You want to make this
world better?

Then help us
                    to help ourselves.

Closed

You closed the school,
Now we have no place to learn.
    I wanted to learn soo
        that heads would turn!
You closed the hospital
we have no place to get medicine
    only thing left is the sick.
You closed the library
and there isn't one book to read
So now I'm
    uneducated
    sick
and ignorant...
You closed the community center
    Now I have to stay in these drug-infested streets
So now I'm
    uneducated
    sick
    ignorant
and a victim of drugs...
You closed my building
My family has no place to stay
We deserved better!
    So now,
I'm uneducated
  sick
  ignorant
  a victim of drugs
and homeless...
Last of all,

you closed the doors to my future
I've become
uneducated
sick
ignorant
a victim of drugs
homeless
and hopeless
I've become the future of tomorrow.

Find Me A Hero

Find me a hero
just a hero to guide me well
someone who's been through
my h*ll.
Gimmie a hero
cause I work so hard
Feel like a junkie,
gimmie my fix!
Find me a hero
someone who'll
teach me
Someone who'll
love me
Someone who'll
help me learn
A Hero
to hold me up
Lord knows I'm tired
spirit knows I'm weak
Was it like this for you?
A hapless poem
a musicless song?
gotta get me a hero
gotta find me a hero
Lord, Lord...
Lord.
Guess I always did!
I needed someone to love me
you gave me a family
Needed someone to guide me,

you gave me Jesus.
Needed someone to support me
keep me strong
you gave me a mother's love.
Needed someone to look up to
you showed me truth
All that I'll ever need
is inside of me.
Guess I didn't need a hero after all!

Young Child

There is a love
for you
young child.
There, There **is** a
love for you
hear what I say?
I know my words
may hurt you
I know I should
watch for what I say.
Deep in my heart,
I do love you
know this,
and go your way.
Please my child,
please forgive me
when I have mean things to say.

Do this,
and seek tomorrow's today.

There is a love for you young child,
Remember what I say.

Beauty

Beauty
Spring 97

My Beauty

My beauty, My beauty, My beauty
    does not come from the straightness of my hair
    nor the lipstick I wear.

My beauty, My beauty, My beauty
    comes from the way that I walk
    and the way that I talk
    the curve of my lips
    and the dip in my hips.

My beauty, My beauty, My beauty
    does not come from the earrings in my ear
    or the clothing I wear
    nor the length of my hair.

My beauty, My beauty, My beauty
    does not come from the lightness of my skin
    but the richness within.

My beauty, My beauty, My beauty
    comes from the thickness of my hair
    the nose on my face
    and everything in its natural place.

My beauty, My beauty, My beauty
    comes from the smile on my face
    and my movements of grace
    my family's care
    and my ancestors everywhere.

My beauty, My beauty, My beauty
    can't be bought in a store
    on no shopping mall floor.

I look at you there
burning your hair
coloring your face
denying your race.

In Me

There is a beauty in me
    something special,
never to be reproduced.

There is a sexuality in me
    something strong,
not defined by
    the clothes I wear
or the style of my hair.

There is a danger in me
    no need for knives or guns
I have my tongue.

There is an energy about me
    all natural
no need for drugs or alcohol.

There is an innocence
    a freedom from iniquity
the gift my Creator
    has given to me.

There's beauty in me
sexuality in me
strength in me
grace in me
danger in me
energy in me
innocence in me

How could you ever forget what's special about me?

Nothing But Beauty

There is nothing but beauty in me.
Scratches may rest on my face,
but it does not slow my grace.
There is nothing but beauty in me.

Love/Relationships

My Love at Rest
Sept, 2000

I Look At You..

I look at you
wanting to kiss
your neck
touch your face.
I look at you
wanting to feel your lips
press against
all of me.
I look at you
look at your eyes
words needed to be said
go ahead,   say them
I won't laugh
won't even smile.
I look at you
imagine a relationship
between you and me
two strong minds
pounding against
one another
Funny how the things that sew
us together
tear us apart.
So,
I look at you.

Of A Woman

Here now, ain't this sexy
feeling my arms and legs
wrapped around
you
like a rope
squeezing out excitement.
Here now, ain't that sexy
feeling my lips
walk down your back
feeling a tongue caress
your hips.
There now, ain't that sexy
feeling a mouth
tantalize
your most private parts
There now, ain't that sexy
Feel the power of a woman
seductively innocent
like a cat's full grown kitten
ready to pounce
Feel the power of a woman...
sweat highlighting your face
as you rest in my arms
peacefully.
There now, ain't that sexy.

All Alone

There you are my Friend, Former Love, all alone, full of pain and anger. And your brother, filled with his own rage, angrily destroying what both you and he needs.

Oh, you must be so frightened, existing on this world without feeling the love of your mother or that of your father.

Little Child, looking for answers and wisdom, but too lost to find them. Former Love, unable to find Peace. Unable to function with Drugs, yet not able to live without them.

My Friend, I hurt so deeply for you. You, on the path to suicide. So sure you are Alone, Unloved, Uncared for, but my Friend, that is not true. Your are Loved, Cared for and Fretted over, by Us, your Friends.

Beautiful Child, stop looking to Other women for the love of your Mother. Release that pain which sends you plummeting through this waste of life.

I feel so for you, till I fall to tears, chasing away my hunger and colour.

Did you know I prayed for you in church this morning? I sent a prayer for you straight to God, in my mind. And when I went to the Alter, the Pastor blessed me, a blessing meant for you. How did he know we both were in need?

Did you know Old love, there is a God? Yes! Yes!!! There is a God! And He loves you, has always known and loved You! Open your soul to Him. You are much too weak to carry this burden alone. You yourself have said.

Precious Heart, I have found a way for you. Take my hand, let me introduce you to your True Father, let Him set your life correct. There are so many gifts He can give to you. Are you ready to love Him?

My friend, we love you. You are not alone, were never alone. Let us help you to find your way.

How Many Times

How many times will you lie?
Listen as my feelings for you die.
How many times will you snare
your dreams?
I know you're hurtin, hurtin deep.
Don't you know I see it in the
way you talk,
the way you walk?
I offered my love to you,
Do you know how it feels to have your love
rejected?
To watch as your heart unwillingly turns to stone?
What do you hide?
Why do you hide?
Why try to hide?

I am someone with whom you could share:
all your dreams
agonies
all your heartfelt desires
How many times will you lie?

The Secret Game

I have a friend. A friend who carries a
dreadful secret.
A secret game.
She came to me one day,
in total disarray.
Her eyes were swollen, her words spoken
small. Spoken in a childlike
manner.
She called people names
did foolish things,
reminiscent of her childhood days.
People flocked from all over
to talk to her.
For she had reached the point
of sheer dismay
sobbing in unidentifiable tears.
Then she looked up at all of us
and said
Ha! Ha! I fooled you!

Aching Heart

The dam is about to break
        How much more do I have to ache.
Past loves have been ripped away
        Past loves have gone astray.
Cried all my cries
        laughed all my laughs
Now emptiness fills me like
        clouds fill the sky.
But do not be mistaken!
        I can hide my face just as
quick as the earth can quake.

Ooh, my aching heart.
        How do I soothe what I do not understand?

Here I Am

Here I am, all alone
A heart full of love
with no place to go.
Where are you Mr. Right?
        My family falls apart
        Past loves trample my heart
        my eyes are brown
        Yet I feel the blues.
If only you knew
All that I suffer through
where is my Romeo?
I'll gladly be your Juliette.

Wrapped in Beauty

Wrapped in beauty,
        dazzled by your light
kiss and love me
        Deep in the night
Kiss me tenderly
        hold me tight
tell me you love me
        Caress me light.
Keep me in your warmth
        love me with your grace
as I kiss all the tears
        From your face.
Dress me with your beauty
        dazzle me with your light
as I kiss and love you
        Till morn's light.

You

Lately,
just lately
I've been thinking about you.
When
I lay down at night,
with my face towards the sky,
I feel you.
Remembering the strength and warmth
in your kiss
The way your
hand
loves my
face.
The way you hold me
The way you...love me?
Oh it doesn't matter!
I have you!
You with the knee shaking kiss
you,
I swear
I've never
felt this way before...
and lately
just lately you've been on my mind.
Feeling satisfaction in my life
happiness with you..
Love?
And I wonder if I'm feeling
something
greater than love itself!

Remember

Remember the smell,
    the scent of the woman
that filled your nostrils
    and placed a smile upon your lips.
Remember how I held you in my arms
    How gently I kissed your cheek,
How I cared for you
    when you were weak.
Remember how I loved you
    when your dreams
were just dreams.
    How I caressed your face
how I relaxed you
    teased you
and needed you.
    When the day comes
that you hold my ashes
    remember all this
and nothing more.
    Then bring my ashes to your lips
and give me a gentle kiss
    smile like you've never smiled before
and toss my ashes
    beyond the shores
where I shall dwell
    forever more.

Reflections

Reflections
Spring 97

A Revelation

I hold this little light
inside my hand.
At first, I didn't even know
I had it!
Imagine me walkin round
with light shinin from me
and not even knowin it!
People told me I was ugly
Blacks called me White
and Whites called me Black
and there were some who
didn't look at all
"your chest is as flat as a wall
and your behind is a floor!"
All that time
still walkin with
this light
"you wanna see me make her cry?
Just watch, she cry easy.."
As the years passed on,
my tears touched my hands,
each time a little more
till one day
I saw this light in my hand
I was able to
make things
and build things.
Suddenly
I WAS BEAUTIFUL
Call me Black or White

cause I'm more than that
I'm a ME
and that's pretty rare around these parts.
And my chest and my behind
fit my body just fine
thank you!
What would happen
if I stopped crying?
Only did it to feed yo ego anyway

Man look at this light
shinin off a me,
workin on gettin my College Degree

get some sunglasses
this light so bright
almost ready to knock out the sun!
Na Uh,
move back
don't you block me!
Not while this here light
steady shinin
in
on
around
and off a me!

Am I Ready

Am I ready
        to say goodbye
to the friends
I've come to love
to the teachers
        I just met?

Am I ready
        to say goodbye
to everything I've known?

Am I ready
        to be the Woman
I was meant to be?

Am I ready
        to leave
                this world behind
                my love behind
                my memories behind?
Am I ready
        to make my own world?
Can I
        handle the independence?
Despite all the h*ll I've
                        given
my mother
my teachers
my friends
myself

Am I ready to say goodbye?

Ambition

I want more
Written articles
grown as a leader
expressed myself
learned the Creator's power
felt my weakness
drew upon my strength
learned to love
learned to cry
Bid farewell to the dead...Goodbye
I have dreamed
and I have sung
earned my place
learned my grace
fallen in love
found the fake
then learned to differentiate
I want more! I want more!
I'm not satisfied
as I continue to strive
I want more! I want more!
I want it all!
I'm not just gonna survive
I wanna thrive!

Why?

I feel so alone, and I don't
know why.
Sometimes I ask myself,
Why? Why are things the way they are?
Why are people so evil?
As my body changes and my mind grows,
I am filled with a sadness
deep inside my soul.
No matter how hard I've tried
I just can't let go.
Sometimes I wonder,
am I really alone?
Is there someone in distant
Lands crying out my pains?
Pains that I bury so
deep inside..

Ever So Pure

White snow on the ground,
ever so profound.
Tree branches reaching and grabbing,
frosted over in ice.
Giving beautiful sights
to the passerbyers
of the night.
White powder filling the streets,
where gay children,
young and old run rampant
and greet every snowflake
with a kiss,
and bid good tidings
to every
Miss.

Hard To Do

What do you do
        when you're not the person you once knew
When your soul is ripped from you?

How do you handle all that anger
        that's just 'bout to explode,
How do you regain your self-control?
Look at that chile
        being forced into womanhood
Look at her smile and
        pretend like nothing's new,
                growing up's so hard to do.
What do you say
when your family
        becomes strange to you
when illusions become the things you thought true?
growin up's so hard to do.
Look at that mother
                heart's so cold
sold that chile for it's weight in gold.
Now don't cry chile,
cause I thought you knew

growing up's so hard to do.

The Value of Life

The value of life,
What does it mean to me?
So much more than your eyes
Can see.

Life, how sweet are thee!
A chance for all that is
Meant to be.

Ask good Life, How do you view?
: Through souls that these hands
Drew.

And fair Life, What do you say?
: Cherish me now
Cause you'll die one day.

Lady of light,
Air of my Lungs
Bring joy into this space.
Bring peace
When you remove us from this place.

Race

Conflict
Aug, 2000

Children

I saw children
I saw children

   laughing, playing
singing, dancing

I saw children
I saw children

   ranting, screaming
shouting

I saw children
   being taught lies
   being brainwashed

I saw Black children
   believing that their minds,
  because of their skin,
to be inferior.

I saw children
   Queens, Kings
all the markings of a Nubian aristocracy

I saw children
I saw Black children
   hated, socially
economically, politically, mutilated

Quick to call 'em
"niggers, half breeds, drug addicts,
worthless Black-skinned apes"
But all I see are children.

Anger Burning

There's a fever burning
hear what I say
there's a fire flaming
a rage mounting
I ain't gonna take it no mo
There's a Black fist raised
Hear what I say
feel my angry fist raised
I ain't gonna take it no mo
Too many have died
Too many wronged,
treated like spit's spit.

In A Different War

It ain't bout color gainst color
Black white green yellow
It ain't bout
gettin equal rights
It ain't bout what you thought it was
There's a bigger struggle
there's a greater trouble
Can you handle the challenge:
Conquer your fears
Can you learn to show respect
fo you self
Can you love
yo-self
stop pimpin
yo-self
Poisonin yo-self
hatin yo-self
killin yo-self.
We can't even love ourselves
let alone
one another
We use guns
for peace
We're so afraid to speak out
shout out
scream out
like the Holy Ghost
got ya
Lord knows it got me.
We's in a march now

long
long road
How strong are you?
Can't be tired
can't be weary
cause we's in a
different war now!

My Chile, My Chile

My chile, My chile
I brought you into this world
without shame
and accepted you
despite your strangeness
I placed upon your neck
my aesthetics
you placed around my neck
a chain.

My bracelets of knowledge dangled from your wrists
while ropes of slavery hung from mine
I dressed you with the fine robes of my culture, dance,
and placed in your right hand the sword of worship.
You dressed me in shifts of the inferior, and gave me torture,
bitterness, and placed in my hand
nothing.

My chile, My chile
You deny me as your mother
you anger and hurt me so
but I do not forget
you are still my child,
afraid of a well deserved spanking.

Mother Africa

Dolly Dolly

Little Black Dolly perched high on my consciousness
        Tell me Dolly Dolly, Do you sing?
Yeah Chile, yeah I sing
        Dolly Dolly, What do you sing?
Chile, I sings of Broken hopes
and dreams unborn
        Dolly Dolly, Do you dance?
Yeah I dance. That's my whole world.
        Your whole world?
Yes, my whole world.
        Dolly Dolly, Why do you sing, Why do you dance?
To remove the pains of life
To cry without crying
        Dolly Dolly, what you got to cry for? Silly Dolly,
        you ain't got nothing to worry bout!
Fool girl, you don't know what you talkin bout.
I's you conscience. I cry yo troubles.
I carry yo guilt!
Nothing to cry bout, Lord if she only knew!
Chile must be fool!

Mirror, Mirror

Mirror, mirror on the wall
Who is the fairest of them all?
Magic Mirror said to me
It clearly is not you!
Look at your color
look at your hue!
Look little Black girl, you ain't nothin cute
you wanna be fair
Change your eyes,
Bleach your skin
Straighten your hair
Not just anyone can look in my mirror.

Religion

Choir
Aug, 2000

God Has Given

I have a voice. God has given me
a voice.
There are days when words fill
my body,
and if I don't let them out
I feel as though I might
burst!
God has meant for me to sing.
God has meant for me to be somebody,
Indeed, He has given me a body.
With this body I can speak many tongues,
He has given me tears to cry
when
I'm sad
when
I'm troubled
when
I'm joyous.
Indeed, God has planned something
for me.

The Sugar Tasted Sweet

Run, chile, run!
        Everybody yells.
Why I got to run?
        I's tired of running
        my feets is weary.
Push on, Push on!
        Everybody shouts.
        But tell that to my legs that's bout to give out!
Move on, move on!
        Everybody screams
        Be strong, chase your dreams.
Along the way I sees Jesus.
        "Tell me Lord, is it worth it on
the other side?"
And he said to me
        "Believe in me, and I will make you strong.
I'll fill your palates with the sweetest of sugars!"
And then we drank together.
So I ran and I ran.
To this day I's still runnin.
People often ask me
        "Ain't you tired yet?'
        "Why you keep going?"
        "Why not give up?"
But when I tell em my answer,
        they look at me in such
shock and awe.
        "What?" they say
                "The sugar tasted sweet?" another say
Lord knows it did!

No Shame

When the tears slowly
roll down my cheek
I have no shame
I'll cry His name.
When my heart's in pain
and
When pain's no thang!
I'll have no shame
I'll cry His name.
When times are tough
and tempers high,
I'll have no shame
I'll cry His name.
When my heart gives way
and my soul starts to fly,
I'll have no shame
I'll sing His name.

Heavenly Father

There lies in me
hope

My Father has set me free.
There lies in me
Knowledge

My Father has given to me.
Heavenly Father
Be my guide
help me to see.

Heavenly Father
Be my strength
make, make me strong
Teach me your way
help me understand

Heavenly Father
of things great and small
Help me to love
Help me to learn.

Just Like The Song Say

Just like the song say,
I still have joy.
Oh Lord, I have laughed
shedded a
many tears
But Lord; you brought me to see
another year.
Just like the song say,
I've come too far
too far, to turn around.

Lord if I haven't cried enough
Good God, I've been tried enough
Brought me from a mighty long way,
so I could meet this day.
Oh Lord,
despite all the years,
anger and tears,
After all the things I've been through
What did that song say?
I still have joy.

Hunger

The Face of Hunger
Sept, 2000

Sleepless Night

Hungry for knowledge
Desire's burning so deep.
There are no books to read,
no words to write.
What good is a pen without ink?
There are no words to sing,
I am a heart without a song!
Lonely, abandoned heart.
Nothing but a sleepless dream.
Meandering in sheer misery,
Yearning to learn about myself,
my history.
Somebody help me!
Somebody teach me!
Somebody love me!
Or will you leave me here
in a sleepless night?

Wordless Song

There's a song that burns
so deep inside of me.
A song that brings tears to my eyes.
I want to sing, so badly
but the words always fail me.
I hum to you this song,
a song that flows so strong.
There's a song that I yearn to sing
But the words, my voice cannot bring
I sit there and hum
this song without words or music.
The song in my heart.

"Poetics"

Poetics
Aug, 2000

Humpty Dumpty

"Humpty Dumpty sat on a wall.
Humpty Dumpty had a great fall."
None of his soldiers,
none of his men
tried to put Humpty together again.

A Hustler ran and got his tools.
He then sold Humpty's shells
as jewels.
A Poor man came and put on
his clothes.
The Devil came and collected
his soul.
A Black man ran for
a frying pan.
That morning the village ate
eggs, grits and ham.

Black Cat

A Black cat crossed my path today,
I says a black cat crossed my path today.
I's wonderin, you know how dey say,
Crossin a Black cat can messup yo day.
Shoot ain't no scrawny cat gonna get in my way.

Well now, my day just rolls on by
don'tcha know I wanna cry!
On my way to school I tripped on a skate
got to my class forty minutes late.

Done cussed out my guy
don'tcha know
I'm readta cry
cause that mangy cat done passed me by.
I yelled at my friends,
done tole off my boss
by the end of the day,
my job I done lost.
Don'tcha know I'm readta die
since that mangy cat done passed me by.

Only Their Momma

A real strong-headed
woman can be dangerous.
You know who I'm talking bout.
The type where only their momma can
tell em the earth's round.
        Oh yeah, these women
can really fool ya.
Be all "sugar and spice"
till they get their eye on a prize,
then LOOK OUT
Yawl fellows best ta watch
out for those strong-headed
women....
and their mommas!

Little Sparrow

Little Sparrow
    you no longer sing
    you no longer fly
Little Sparrow
    where's the beauty in your eye?
    you no longer hunt
I wonder if you even breathe!
What happened to your nest?
Fit for the dead to be laid to rest!
Little Sparrow
            where is the melody
to your song?
The pride in your wing,
where has all this gone?
            Why do you lie still and rust?
Your place of living is
nothing more than dust.
Little Sparrow
do not let yourself die...
Little Sparrow....
    you no longer fly.

True Blue

After I've gone,
what will you say of me?

I've taken your children
and made them my own.

I gave them my love,
and loved them as if they came from my womb.

I gave them my discipline,
and made them open their eyes and question the things they were
told not to question.

And my final gift to them,
I leave a part of my self.
How much of that will you remember?

Will you remember the first day I met you,
how I embraced you with warmth and kindness

And how I sometimes treated you better than I treated myself?

Will you remember how I sat you down and consoled you
and listened to you
and laughed with you
and loved you as my Aunts and Uncles
as my brothers and my sisters?

After I leave,
what will you say of me?

Expressive Me

Such a mature young man,
forced to watch
a lying plan.
Full of love, swallowed by woe,
learning bitterly
that you reap what you sow.

Harlem

Riding the subway, hands on my head
I remember Harlem, **My** Harlem..long dead.

Nappy-headed kids runnin round
playing
with
crack vials, like leaves..EVERYWHERE

Men broken down, old and cold
trapped in their own
eternal failures

Those babies, with nothing to drink
but powdered milk.

Therefore,
my children grew with food
unmade by me
In a Paradise's Ghetto
we were too blind to see.

So wanting in respect, we destroy one another.

The Good Word

It really was a simple mistake!
My friend always said it
We'd all grin
        cause she said the forbidden
Secretly in our hearts,
        we tingled
                        an unknown ecstacy
confusing a child with the accepted
and the forbidden.

During a big family dinner
                        my cousin, the dancing wonder
doing some crazy dance.
        I planned.
It was the accepted word "HECK" My Savior
my impunity.
"Marlene, what the HELL are you doing?"
NO! NO! NO! The WRONG one!
A sharp quick light
At the end was my mother
angry, red, and breathing hard.
But I was in a daze.
The sheer ecstacy.
The tongue of my mouth
touching it's roof, producing the H-E-L.
Then moving seductively down
to form that lasting L.

My Grandma found out
"I didn't know you could talk like that"

such a disappointed tone.
A word of this,
I HEARD NOT!
How brave I was to speak!
giddiness overcame me
(In the privacy of my room.
I was brave, not a fool!)
planning my next adventure.

Eye See

I see it all,
little babies full of hunger
the persuasions of the gun
the grasping for a power
        we know we can never have.
Pro-lifers killing life
the turmoils and strife.
Eye see it all
Cold, cause I don't care,
my heart already numbed
the sympathy having been burned away.
Eye see it all
Everything
Nothing is hidden from me!
Hm Hm, I'm a god!
Not the original,
but a god nonetheless
Cause Eye see it all.
My church,
that humble place of worship
is my T.V.
There is a communion
with my remote,
Welcoming various faces into my home
daily.
Nothing is hidden from me.
In darkness,
        the truth comes from my T.V. light.
Won't you come and have fellowship
with me?

To Be A Woman

It must be tough to be a boy
growing to a man.
But it's hard to be a girl
growing into a woman.
When we're on the trains,
walking by, or just relaxin
and a PACK of boys happen to be near,
We're no longer human.
Suddenly a girl with lungs becomes
meat to be devoured.
Some piece of merchandise
about to be auctioned off and what-not.
    We have to watch the type of clothing we wear around you
fellas.
If the skirt's too short, the blouse too revealing or the pants too tight, then we're asking for a
"(smooch) Come here baby, Papa got somethin for ya"
and Lord if there ain't some fool who thinks not only did you
dress for him, but he got the right to sample the goods!
    Do I look like some Welfare cheese? What you think, I'm just givin it away?
It must be hard changing
from boys to Men. But it's a job
for girls learning to be women.
If we have too many boyfriends,
then we're h-o-e-s.
If it's rumored we had sex with some guy,
then we're s-l-u-t-s.

If we're moody,
then we must be P.M.Sing.
And when we refuse to give into your demands,
we're b*tches.
And when we don't feel like being touched by you,
then we're d-y-k-e-s.
And when we talk about your stupid-a** mistakes,
then we're gossips and s-k-a-n-k-s.
It must be hard growing from a boy to a man,
but it's a f*cking 24 hour job for a girl to be a woman.

Stretch Out Your Hands

Africa,
        when will you stretch out your hands to me?
After years of struggle,
        I am still but a nigger
Brutalized so,
        till I can't help but remember
the promise of Africa,
        why have you abandoned me?
when can I reclaim my ancestry?
Oh Africa,
        stretch out your hands to me.
I am a soul,
        longing for rest
return me to the land
my forefathers hath blest.
        I live in the Americas, and Europe
dominated by devils who continue
to do us wrong.
Oh Africa,
        let me build in thee
and make you strong
I am your resource
longing for home
It was we who shaped Europe and the Americas,
we the children of you,
children so lost
till we walk confused
we hate the wool you placed
upon our heads,
we walk around with inferior hair

upon which false beauty is fed.
We place superiority on those of lighter skin
and try to devalue
the Blackness within.
Oh Africa,
          when will you call for me,
do I not deserve to be free?
Our men are broken, beaten and scorned
it is with blood that this mighty race mourns.
When will you soothe us
with your mighty arms?
Oh Africa,
          have you forgotten me?

www.ingramcontent.com/pod-product-compliance
Ingram Content Group UK Ltd.
Pitfield, Milton Keynes, MK11 3LW, UK
UKHW041936190726
13854UKWH00004B/1619

9 780759 601338